Find It in Nature!

Fish

by Jenna Lee Gleisner

Bullfrog Books

Ideas for Parents and Teachers

Bullfrog Books let children practice reading informational text at the earliest reading levels. Repetition, familiar words, and photo labels support early readers.

Before Reading
- Discuss the cover photo. What does it tell them?
- Look at the picture glossary together. Read and discuss the words.

Read the Book
- "Walk" through the book and look at the photos. Let the child ask questions. Point out the photo labels.
- Read the book to the child, or have them read independently.

After Reading
- Prompt the child to think more. Ask: Have you ever seen a fish? What did it look like?

Bullfrog Books are published by Jump!
5357 Penn Avenue South
Minneapolis, MN 55419
www.jumplibrary.com

Copyright © 2025 Jump! International copyright reserved in all countries. No part of this book may be reproduced in any form without written permission from the publisher.

Library of Congress Cataloging-in-Publication Data

Names: Gleisner, Jenna Lee, author.
Title: Fish / by Jenna Lee Gleisner.
Description: Minneapolis, MN: Jump!, Inc., [2025]
Series: Find it in nature! | Includes index.
Audience: Ages 5–8
Identifiers: LCCN 2024023339 (print)
LCCN 2024023340 (ebook)
ISBN 9798892136969 (hardcover)
ISBN 9798892136976 (paperback)
ISBN 9798892136983 (ebook)
Subjects: LCSH: Freshwater fishes—Juvenile literature.
Classification: LCC QL624 .G54 2025 (print)
LCC QL624 (ebook)
DDC 597.176—dc23/eng/20240522
LC record available at https://lccn.loc.gov/2024023339
LC ebook record available at https://lccn.loc.gov/2024023340

Editor: Katie Chanez
Designer: Molly Ballanger

Photo Credits: Eric Isselee/Shutterstock, cover; FedBul/Shutterstock, 1, 22bmr; kzww/Shutterstock, 3; Krzysztof Odziomek/Shutterstock, 4; Judy M Darby/Shutterstock, 5; Griffin Gillespie/Shutterstock, 6–7, 23bl; LaSalle-Photo/iStock, 8–9, 23tl, 23tr, 23br; Roberto Nistri/Alamy, 10–11, 23tm; blickwinkel/Alamy, 12; Chase D'animulls/Shutterstock, 13; Eduardo Baena/iStock, 14–15; Michael Wood/Dreamstime, 16–17; Rostislav Stefanek/Shutterstock, 18; FedBul/iStock, 19; George Grall/Alamy, 20–21; Dan Thornberg/Shutterstock, 22tl, 22tr; azure1/Shutterstock, 22tml; Joe_Potato/iStock, 22tmr; andyKRAKOVSKI/iStock, 22bl; Sergey Goruppa/Shutterstock, 22bml; IrinaK/Shutterstock, 22br; dimdiz/Shutterstock, 23bm; Oleksandr Kliuiev/Shutterstock, 24.

Printed in the United States of America at Corporate Graphics in North Mankato, Minnesota.

Table of Contents

Gills and Fins	4
Match the Fish	22
Picture Glossary	23
Index	24
To Learn More	24

Gills and Fins

Fish swim.

They live in water.
Let's find fish!

Fish breathe with gills.
Bluegills have dark spots.
Where?
By their gills!

Walleye scales are light.
They have black bands.
Two dorsal fins stick up.
One has spines.

A catfish has barbels. Can you guess how it got its name?

A sturgeon has them, too.
It has rows of plates.

It is big!

It jumps out of the water!

Salmon can be many colors.
A sockeye is red!
Its head is green.

Eels are long.
They look like snakes.

A northern pike is long, too.
It is green with white spots.

It has a big mouth.
See its teeth?

This fish mouth is bigger!
It is a bass.
Open up!

Match the Fish

Match each fish with its name. Look back at the book if you need help!

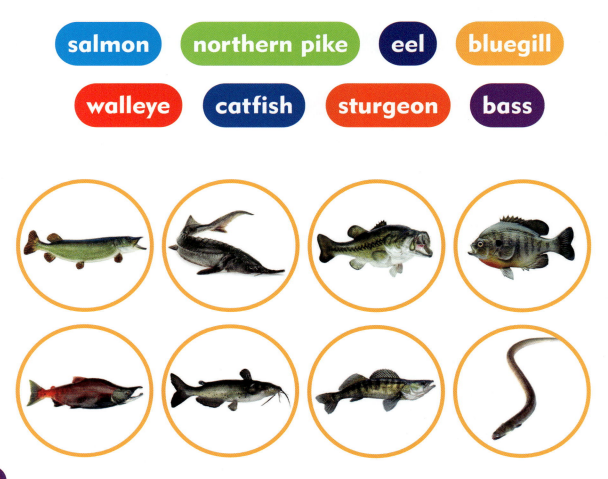

Picture Glossary

bands
Stripes of color.

barbels
Whisker-like feelers near a fish's mouth that help it taste and feel.

dorsal fins
Flat, thin fins on top of fish bodies that help them balance.

gills
Organs fish have that filter oxygen out of water to breathe.

scales
Thin, flat pieces of hard skin that cover the bodies of most fish.

spines
Hard, sharp points.

Index

barbels 10
bass 20
bluegills 6
catfish 10
eels 17
mouth 19, 20
northern pike 18
plates 12
scales 9
sockeye 14
sturgeon 12
walleye 9

To Learn More

Finding more information is as easy as 1, 2, 3.

❶ Go to www.factsurfer.com

❷ Enter "fish" into the search box.

❸ Choose your book to see a list of websites.